The Word

The Most Powerful Word Ever Spoken

The Teachings of Jesus in Luke, Mark and Matthew

VICTOR BOOKS

A DIVISION OF SCRIPTURE PRESS PUBLICATIONS INC.
USA CANADA ENGLAND

Contents

THE WORD 2
**The Teachings of Jesus
in Luke**

Copyright © 1994 by Victor Books/SP Publications, Inc. Original edition published in
 Denmark under the title, THE WORD, The Teachings of Jesus in Luke, Mark
 and Matthew by Scandinavia Publishing House, Copenhagen, Denmark.
 Copyright © 1993 Scandinavia Publishing House.
Text Copyright © Holy Bible, New International Version®, 1973, 1978, 1984 by
 International Bible Society. Used by permission of Zondervan Publishing House.
 All rights reserved.

ISBN: 1-56476-254-8

1 2 3 4 5 6 7 8 9 10 Printing/Year 98 97 96 95 94

Printed in Singapore

Preface

In the beginning was the Word,
and the Word was with God,
and the Word was God.
He [Jesus] was with God in the beginning.
Through him all things were made;
without him nothing was made that has been made.

John 1:1-3

By the word of the LORD were the heavens made,
their starry host by the breath of his mouth.
He gathers the waters of the sea into jars;
he puts the deep into storehouses.
Let all the earth fear the LORD;
let all the people of the world revere him.
For he spoke, and it came to be;
he commanded, and it stood firm.

Psalm 33:6-9

He is the image of the invisible God,
the firstborn over all creation.
For by him all things were created:
things in heaven and on earth, visible and invisible,
whether thrones or powers or rulers or authorities;
all things were created by him and for him.
He is before all things,
and in him all things hold together.

Colossians 1:15-17

In these last days he has spoken to us by his Son,
whom he appointed heir of all things,
and through whom he made the universe.
The Son is the radiance of God's glory
and the exact representation of his being,
sustaining all things by his powerful word.

Hebrews 1:2-3

3

Jesus Sends Out
the Seventy-two

Luke 10:1-16

After this the Lord appointed seventy-two others and sent them two by two ahead
of him to every town and place where he was
about to go. He told them,

The harvest is plentiful, but the workers are few.
Ask the Lord of the harvest, therefore, to send out workers into his
harvest field.
Go! I am sending you out like lambs among wolves.
Do not take a purse or bag or sandals; and do not greet anyone on the road.

When you enter a house, first say,
"Peace to this house."
If a man of peace is there, your peace will rest on him;
if not, it will return to you.
Stay in that house, eating and drinking whatever they give you, for the worker
deserves his wages. Do not move around from house to house.

When you enter a town and are welcomed, eat what is set before you.
Heal the sick who are there and tell them, "The kingdom of God is near you."
But when you enter a town and are not
welcomed, go into its streets and say,
"Even the dust of your town that sticks to our feet we wipe off against you.

Yet be sure of this:
The kingdom of God is near."
I tell you,
it will be more bearable on that day for Sodom than for that town.
Woe to you, Korazin! Woe to you, Bethsaida!
For if the miracles that were performed in you had been performed
in Tyre and Sidon,
they would have repented long ago, sitting in sackcloth and ashes.
But it will be more bearable for Tyre and Sidon at the judgment than for you.
And you, Capernaum, will you be lifted up to the skies?
No, you will go down to the depths.
He who listens to you listens to me; he who rejects you rejects me;
but he who rejects me rejects him who sent me.

The Seventy-two Return with Joy

Luke 10:17-20

The seventy-two returned with joy and said,
"Lord, even the demons submit to us in your name."
He replied,

I saw Satan fall like lightning from heaven.

I have given you authority to trample on snakes and scorpions and to overcome all the power of the enemy; nothing will harm you.

However, do not rejoice that the spirits submit to you,

but rejoice that your names are written in heaven.

Jesus Rejoices in the Spirit

Luke 10:21-24

At that time Jesus, full of joy through the Holy Spirit, said,

I praise you, Father, Lord of heaven and earth, because you have hidden these things from the wise and learned, and revealed them to little children. Yes, Father, for this was your good pleasure.

All things have been committed to me by my Father. No one knows who the Son is except the Father, and no one knows who the Father is except the Son and those to whom the Son chooses to reveal him.

Then he turned to his disciples and said privately,

Blessed are the eyes that see what you see. For I tell you that many prophets and kings wanted to see what you see but did not see it, and to hear what you hear but did not hear it.

The Lamp of the Body

Luke 11:33-36

No one
lights a lamp
and puts it in a place
where it will be hidden,
or under a bowl.
Instead
he puts it on its stand,
so that those who come
in may see the light.

Your eye is the lamp
of your body.
When your eyes
are good,
your whole body also
is full of light.
But when they are bad,
your body also
is full of darkness.

See to it, then, that
the light within you
is not darkness.

Therefore,
if your whole body
is full of light,
and no part of it
dark,
it will be
completely lighted,
as when the light of a
lamp shines on you.

Six Woes

Luke 11:37-52

When Jesus had finished speaking,
a Pharisee invited him to eat with him;
so he went in and reclined at the table.
But the Pharisee, noticing that Jesus
did not first wash before the meal,
was surprised.
Then the Lord said to him,

*Now then, you Pharisees clean
the outside of the cup and dish, but
inside you are full of greed
and wickedness.
You foolish people!
Did not the one who made the
outside make the inside also?
But give what is inside the dish to
the poor, and everything will be clean
for you.*

Woe to you Pharisees,
*because you give God a tenth of
your mint, rue and all other kinds of
garden herbs, but you neglect justice
and the love of God. You should have
practiced the latter without leaving
the former undone.*

Woe to you Pharisees,
*because you love the
most important seats in the
synagogues and greetings in the
marketplaces.*

Woe to you,
*because you are like unmarked
graves, which men walk over without
knowing it.*
One of the experts in the law answered
him, "Teacher, when you say these
things, you insult us also."

Jesus replied,
And you experts in the law,
woe to you,
*because you load people down
with burdens they can hardly
carry,
and you yourselves will not lift one
finger to help them.*

Woe to you,
*because you build tombs
for the prophets, and it was your
forefathers who killed them.
So you testify that you approve of
what your forefathers did; they
killed the prophets, and you
build their tombs.
Because of this,
God in his wisdom said,
"I will send them prophets and
apostles, some of whom they will
kill and others they will
persecute."*

*Therefore this generation will be
held responsible for the blood of
all the prophets that has been
shed since the beginning
of the world,
from the blood of Abel to the blood
of Zechariah, who was killed
between the altar and the
sanctuary. Yes, I tell you, this
generation will be held responsible
for it all.*

Woe to you
*experts in the law, because you
have taken away the key to
knowledge. You yourselves have
not entered, and you have
hindered those who were entering.*

Beware of Hypocrisy

Luke 12:1-3

Meanwhile, when a crowd of many thousands had gathered, so that they were trampling on one another, Jesus began to speak first to his disciples, saying:
Be on your guard against the yeast of the Pharisees, which is hypocrisy.
There is nothing concealed that will not be disclosed, or hidden that will not be made known.
What you have said in the dark will be heard in the daylight, and what you have whispered in the ear in the inner rooms will be proclaimed from the housetops.

Jesus Teaches the Fear of God

Luke 12:4-7

I tell you, my friends, do not be afraid of those who kill the body and after that can do no more.
But I will show you whom you should fear:
Fear him who, after the killing of the body, has power to throw you into hell.
Yes, I tell you, fear him.

Are not five sparrows sold for two pennies? Yet not one of them is forgotten by God.
Indeed, the very hairs of your head are all numbered.
Don't be afraid;
you are worth more than many sparrows.

Confess Christ before Men

Luke 12:8-12

*I tell you,
whoever acknowledges
me before men, the Son
of Man will also
acknowledge him before
the angels
of God.
But he who disowns me
before men will be
disowned before
the angels
of God.
And everyone who
speaks a word against
the Son of Man will be
forgiven,
but anyone who
blasphemes against the
Holy Spirit will not be
forgiven.*

*When you are brought
before synagogues,
rulers, and authorities,
do not worry about how
you will defend
yourselves
or what
you will say,*

**for the Holy Spirit
will teach you at that
time what you
should say.**

The Rich Fool

Luke 12:14-15

Jesus replied, Man, who appointed me a judge or an arbiter between you?

Then he said to them, Watch out! Be on your guard against all kinds of greed;

a man's life does not consist in the abundance of his possessions.

Do Not Worry

Luke 12:22-34

Then Jesus said to his disciples:
*Therefore I tell you, do not worry about your life, what you will
eat; or about your body, what you will wear.
Life is more than food,
and the body more than clothes.*

*Consider the ravens:
They do not sow or reap,
they have no storeroom or barn; yet God feeds them.
And how much more valuable you are than birds!
Who of you by worrying can add a single hour to his life?
Since you cannot do this very little thing, why do you worry
about the rest?*

*Consider how the lilies grow.
They do not labor or spin. Yet I tell you, not even Solomon in all
his splendor was dressed like one of these.
If that is how God clothes
the grass of the field, which is here today, and tomorrow is
thrown into the fire,
how much more will he clothe you, O you of little faith!*

*And do not set your heart on what you will eat or drink;
do not worry about it.
For the pagan world runs after all such things, and your Father
knows that you need them.*

*But seek his kingdom, and these things will be given to you as
well.*

**Do not be afraid, little flock, for your Father has been
pleased to give you the kingdom.**

*Sell your possessions and give to the poor.
Provide purses for yourselves that will not wear out, a treasure
in heaven that will not be exhausted, where no thief comes near
and no moth destroys.*
**For where your treasure is,
there your heart will be also.**

Watchfulness

Luke 12:35-40

Be dressed ready for service and keep your lamps burning, like men waiting for their master to return from a wedding banquet, so that when he comes and knocks they can immediately open the door for him.

It will be good for those servants whose master finds them watching when he comes. I tell you the truth, he will dress himself to serve, will have them recline at the table and will come and wait on them.

It will be good for those servants whose master finds them ready, even if he comes in the second or third watch of the night.

But understand this: If the owner of the house had known at what hour the thief was coming, he would not have let his house be broken into.

You also must be ready, because the Son of Man will come at an hour when you do not expect him.

Discern the Time

Luke 12:54-59

He said to the crowd:
*When you see a cloud
rising in the west,
immediately you say,
"It's going to rain,"
and it does.
And when the south wind
blows, you say,
"It's going to be hot,"
and it is.*

*Hypocrites!
You know how to interpret
the appearance of the
earth and the sky. How is
it that you don't know how
to interpret this present
time?*

**Why don't you
judge for yourselves
what is right?**

*As you are going with your
adversary to the
magistrate, try hard to be
reconciled to him on the
way, or he may drag you
off to the judge,
and the judge turn you
over to the officer,
and the officer
throw you into prison.*

*I tell you, you will not get
out until you have paid the
last penny.*

15

Repent or Perish

Luke 13:1-5

Now there were some present
at that time who told Jesus
about the Galileans whose blood Pilate
had mixed with their sacrifices.
Jesus answered,
*Do you think that these Galileans
were worse sinners than all the other
Galileans because they suffered
this way?
I tell you, no!*
**But unless you repent,
you too will all perish.**
*Or those eighteen who died
when the tower in Siloam fell on
them—do you think they were more
guilty than all the others living
in Jerusalem?
I tell you, no!*
**But unless you repent,
you too will all perish.**

A Spirit of Infirmity

Luke 13:15-17

The Lord answered him,
*You hypocrites! Doesn't each of
you on the Sabbath untie his ox or
donkey from the stall and lead it out
to give it water?
Then should not this woman, a
daughter of Abraham, whom Satan
has kept bound for eighteen long
years, be set free on the Sabbath day
from what bound her?*
When he said this, all his opponents
were humiliated, but the people were
delighted with all the wonderful things
he was doing.

The Narrow Door

Luke 13:23-32

Someone asked him,
"Lord, are only a few people going to be
saved?" He said to them,

*Make every effort to enter through the
narrow door, because many,
I tell you,
will try to enter and will not
be able to.
Once the owner of the house gets up
and closes the door,
you will stand outside knocking
and pleading,
"Sir, open the door for us."
But he will answer, "I don't know you
or where you come from."
Then you will say,
"We ate and drank with you,
and you taught in our streets."
But he will reply,
"I don't know you or where you come
from. Away from me,
all you evildoers!"*

*There will be weeping there,
and gnashing of teeth, when you see
Abraham, Isaac and Jacob
and all the prophets in the kingdom of
God, but you yourselves thrown out.
People will come from east and west
and north and south,
and will take their places
at the feast in the kingdom of God.*

**Indeed there are those
who are last who will be first,
and first who will be last.**

Jerusalem

Luke 13:33

*In any case,
I must keep going
today and tomorrow
and the next day—
for surely
no prophet
can die
outside
Jerusalem!*

Take the Lowly Place

Luke 14:7-14

When he noticed how the guests
picked the places of honor at the table, he
told them this parable:
When someone invites you
to a wedding feast, do not take the
place of honor, for a person more
distinguished than you may have
been invited.
If so,
the host who invited both of you
will come and say to you, "Give this
man your seat." Then, humiliated, you
will have to take the least
important place.
But when you are invited, take the
lowest place, so that when your host
comes, he will say to you, "Friend, move
up to a better place." Then you will be
honored in the presence of all your
fellow guests.
For everyone
who exalts himself
will be humbled, and he who
humbles himself will be exalted.
Then Jesus said to his host,
When you give a luncheon or dinner, do
not invite your friends, your brothers or
relatives, or your rich neighbors; if you
do, they may invite you back and so
you will be repaid.

But when you give a banquet,
invite the poor, the crippled, the
lame, the blind, and you will be
blessed.
Although they cannot repay you,
you will be repaid at the
resurrection of the righteous.

21

The Cost of Being a Disciple

Luke 14:25-35

Large crowds were traveling with Jesus, and turning to them he said:
If anyone comes to me and does not hate his father and mother, his wife and children, his brothers and sisters— yes, even his own life— he cannot be my disciple.

And anyone who does not carry his cross and follow me cannot be my disciple.

Suppose one of you wants to build a tower. Will he not first sit down and estimate the cost to see if he has enough money to complete it?

For if he lays the foundation and is not able to finish it, everyone who sees it will ridicule him, saying, "This fellow began to build and was not able to finish."

Or suppose a king
is about to go to war
against another king.

Will he not first
sit down and consider
whether he is able
with ten thousand men
to oppose the one
coming against him
with twenty thousand?

If he is not able,
he will send a
delegation while the
other is still a long
way off and will ask
for terms of peace.

In the same way,
any of you who does
not give up everything
he has cannot be my
disciple.

Salt is good,
but if it loses its
saltiness, how can it
be made salty again?
It is fit neither for the
soil nor for the manure
pile;
it is thrown out.

**He who has ears
to hear,
let him hear.**

Faithful in Small Things

Luke 16:10-18

*Whoever can be trusted
with very little
can also be trusted
with much, and whoever is dishonest
with very little will also be dishonest
with much.
So if you have not been trustworthy
in handling worldly wealth, who will trust you
with true riches?
And if you have not been trustworthy
with someone else's property,
who will give you property of your own?*

No servant can serve two masters.
*Either he will hate the one and love the other, or
he will be devoted to the one
and despise the other.*
You cannot serve both God and Money.

*The Pharisees, who loved money,
heard all this and were sneering at Jesus.
He said to them,
You are the ones who justify yourselves
in the eyes of men, but God knows your hearts.
What is highly valued among men
is detestable in God's sight.
The Law and the Prophets
were proclaimed until John.
Since that time, the good news of the kingdom
of God is being preached, and everyone is
forcing his way into it.
It is easier for heaven and earth to disappear
than for the least stroke of a pen to drop out of
the Law.
Anyone who divorces his wife and marries
another woman commits adultery,
and the man who marries a divorced woman
commits adultery.*

Sin, Faith, Duty

Luke 17:1-10

Jesus said to his disciples:
Things that cause people to sin are bound to come, but woe to that person through whom they come.
It would be better for him to be thrown into the sea with a millstone tied around his neck than for him to cause one of these little ones to sin.
So watch yourselves. If your brother sins, rebuke him, and if he repents, forgive him.
If he sins against you seven times in a day, and seven times comes back to you and says, "I repent," forgive him.
The apostles said to the Lord, "Increase our faith!"

He replied,
If you have faith
as small as a mustard seed,
you can say to this mulberry tree, "Be uprooted and planted in the sea,"
and it will obey you.

Suppose one of you had a servant plowing or looking after the sheep. Would he say to the servant when he comes in from the field, "Come along now and sit down to eat"?
Would he not rather say, "Prepare my supper, get yourself ready and wait on me while I eat and drink; after that you may eat and drink"?
Would he thank the servant because he did what he was told to do?
So you also, when you have done everything you were told to do, should say, "We are unworthy servants; we have only done our duty."

The Coming of the Kingdom

Luke 17:20-37

Once, having been asked by the Pharisees when the kingdom of God would come, Jesus replied,
*The kingdom of God does not come visibly,
nor will people say, "Here it is," or "There it is," because the kingdom of God is within you.*

*Then he said to his disciples,
The time is coming when you will long to see one of the days of the Son of Man, but you will not see it.
Men will tell you,
"There he is!" or
"Here he is!"
Do not go running off after them.*

For the Son of Man in his day will be like the lightning, which flashes and lights up the sky from one end to the other.

*But first he must suffer many things and be rejected by this generation.
Just as it was in the days of Noah, so also will it be in the days of the Son of Man.*

People were eating, drinking,
marrying and being given in
marriage up to the day
Noah entered the ark.
Then the flood came
and destroyed them all.
It was the same in the days of
Lot. People were
eating and drinking,
buying and selling,
planting and building.
But the day Lot left Sodom, fire
and sulfur rained down from
heaven and destroyed them all.
It will be just like this on the
day the Son of Man is revealed.
On that day no one who is on
the roof of his house,
with his goods inside,
should go down to get them.
Likewise, no one in the field
should go back for anything.
Remember Lot's wife!

**Whoever tries to keep his
life will lose it,
and whoever loses his life
will preserve it.**

I tell you, on that night two
people will be in one bed;
one will be taken and the other
left.
Two women will be grinding
grain together;
one will be taken
and the other left.
"Where, Lord?" they asked. He
replied,
Where there is a dead body,
there the vultures will gather.

Divorce

Matthew 19:3-12 (Mark 10:1-12)

Some Pharisees came to him to test him.
They asked, "Is it lawful for a man to divorce
his wife for any and every reason?"
Haven't you read,
he replied,
*that at the beginning the Creator "made
them male and female,"
and said,
"For this reason a man will leave
his father and mother and be united to his
wife, and the two will become
one flesh"?
So they are no longer two, but one.
Therefore what God has joined together,*
let man not separate.
"Why then," they asked,
"did Moses command that a man give his wife
a certificate of divorce and send her away?"
Jesus replied,
*Moses permitted you to divorce
your wives because your hearts were hard.
But it was not this way from the beginning.
I tell you that anyone who divorces his
wife, except for marital unfaithfulness,
and marries another woman commits
adultery.*

The disciples said to him, "If this is the
situation between a husband and wife, it is
better not to marry."
Jesus replied,

*Not everyone can accept this teaching,
but only those to whom it has been given.
For some are eunuchs because they were
born that way; others were made that way
by men; and others have renounced
marriage because of the kingdom of
heaven. The one who can accept this
should accept it.*

Jesus Counsels the Rich

Mark 10:17-31 (Matthew 19:16-30, Luke 18:18-30)

As Jesus started on his way, a man
ran up to him and
fell on his knees before him. "Good
teacher," he asked,
"what must I do to inherit eternal
life?"
Why do you call me good?
Jesus answered.
No one is good—except God alone.
You know the commandments: "Do
not murder, do not commit adultery,
do not steal, do not give false
testimony, do not defraud, honor
your father and mother."
"Teacher," he declared,
"all these I have kept
since I was a boy."

Jesus looked at him and loved him.
One thing you lack,
he said.
Go, sell everything you have
and give to the poor, and you will
have treasure in heaven. Then
come, follow me.

At this the man's face fell.
He went away sad,
because he had great wealth.
Jesus looked around and said to his
disciples,
How hard it is for the rich to enter
the kingdom of God!

The disciples were amazed at his words. But Jesus said again,

Children, how hard it is to enter the kingdom of God!
It is easier for a camel to go through the eye of a needle than for a rich man to enter the kingdom of God.

The disciples were even more amazed, and said to each other, "Who then can be saved?"

Jesus looked at them and said,

With man this is impossible, but not
with God;
all things are possible with God.

Peter said to him, "We have left everything to follow you!"
I tell you the truth,
Jesus replied,
no one who has left home or brothers or sisters or mother or father or children or fields for me and the gospel
will fail to receive
a hundred times as much in this present age (homes, brothers, sisters, mothers, children and fields—and with them, persecutions)
and in the age to come, eternal life.

But many who are first will be last, and the last first.

Greatness Is Serving

Matthew 20:20-28 (Mark 10:35-45)

Then the mother of Zebedee's sons came to
Jesus with her sons and, kneeling down,
asked a favor of him.

What is it you want?
he asked.
She said, "Grant that one of these two
sons of mine may sit at your right and the
other at your left in your kingdom."
*You don't know what you
are asking,*
Jesus said to them.
*Can you drink the cup I am going
to drink?*
"We can," they answered.
Jesus said to them,
*You will indeed drink from my cup, but
to sit at my right or left is not for me to
grant. These places belong to those for
whom they have been prepared by my
Father.*

When the ten heard about this, they were
indignant with the two brothers.
Jesus called them together and said,

*You know that the rulers
of the Gentiles lord it over them,
and their high officials exercise authority
over them.*
Not so with you.
*Instead, whoever wants to
become great among you
must be your servant,
and whoever wants to be first
must be your slave—
just as the Son of Man
did not come to be served, but to serve,
and to give his life as a ransom for
many.*

Paying Taxes to Caesar

Luke 20:21-26 (Mark 12:13-17, Matthew 22:15-21)

So the spies
questioned him:
"Teacher, we know that
you speak and teach
what is right, and that
you do not show
partiality but teach the
way of God in
accordance with
the truth.
Is it right for us to pay
taxes to Caesar or not?"

He saw through their
duplicity and said
to them,
Show me a denarius.
Whose portrait and
inscription are on it?
"Caesar's,"
they replied.
He said to them,
Then give
to Caesar
what is Caesar's,
and to God
what is God's.

They were unable to
trap him in what he had
said there in public.
And astonished by his
answer, they became
silent.

Marriage at the Resurrection

Luke 20:34-38 (Matthew 22:23-32, Mark 12:18-27)

*The people of this age
marry and are given in
marriage.
But those who are
considered worthy of
taking part in that age
and in the resurrection
from the dead
will neither marry
nor be given in marriage,
and they can no longer
die; for they are like the
angels.
They are God's children,
since they are children of
the resurrection.*

*But in the account
of the bush, even Moses
showed that the dead
rise, for he calls the Lord
"the God of Abraham,
and the God of Isaac,
and the God of Jacob."
He is not the God of the
dead,
but of the living,
**for to him all are
alive.***

The Greatest Commandment

Mark 12:28-31

One of the teachers
of the law came and heard them
debating.
Noticing that Jesus had given
them a good answer,
he asked him,
"Of all the commandments,
which is the most important?"

*The most important one,
answered Jesus,
is this:*

**"Hear, O Israel,
the Lord our God,
the Lord is one.
Love the Lord your God
with all your heart
and with all your soul
and with all your mind
and with all your
strength."**

*The second is this:
"Love your neighbor as
yourself." There is no
commandment greater than
these.*

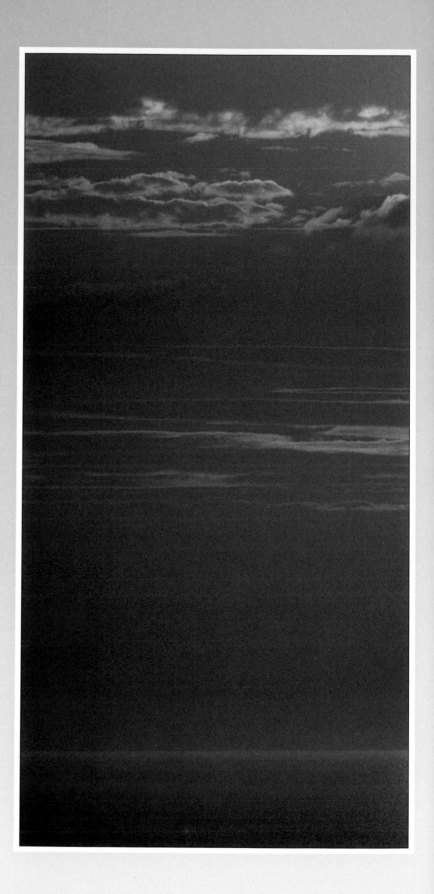

Whose Son Is Christ?

Matthew 22:41-46 (Mark 12:35-37, Luke 20:41-44)

While the Pharisees were gathered together, Jesus asked them,

What do you think about the Christ? Whose son is he?

"The son of David," they replied.

He said to them,
How is it then that David, speaking by the Spirit, calls him "Lord"?
For he says,
"The Lord said to my Lord:
'Sit at my right hand until I put your enemies under your feet.' "
If then David calls him "Lord,"
how can he be his son?

No one could say a word in reply, and from that day on no one dared to ask him any more questions.

Seven Woes

Matthew 23:1-37

Then Jesus said to the crowds and to his disciples:

The teachers of the law
and the Pharisees
sit in Moses' seat.
So you must obey them
and do everything they tell you.
But do not do what they do, for they
do not practice what they preach.
They tie up heavy loads and put
them on men's shoulders,
but they themselves are not willing
to lift a finger to move them.

Everything they do
is done for men to see: They make
their phylacteries wide and the
tassels on their garments long;
they love the place of honor
at banquets and the
most important seats in the
synagogues;

they love to be greeted in the
marketplaces and to have men
call them "Rabbi."
But you are not to be called "Rabbi,"
for you have only one master and
you are all brothers.
And do not call anyone
on earth "father," for you have one
Father, and he is in heaven.
Nor are you to be called "teacher,"
for you have one Teacher, the Christ.
The greatest among you
will be your servant.
For whoever exalts himself will be
humbled, and whoever humbles
himself will be exalted.

Woe to you,
teachers of the law
and Pharisees, you hypocrites!
You shut the kingdom of heaven in
men's faces. You yourselves do
not enter, nor will you let those
enter who are trying to.

Woe to you,
teachers of the law
and Pharisees, you hypocrites!
You travel over land and sea to
win a single convert, and when he
becomes one, you make him twice
as much a son of hell as you are.

Woe to you,
blind guides! You say, "If anyone
swears by the temple, it means
nothing; but if anyone swears by
the gold of the temple, he is bound
by his oath."
You blind fools!
Which is greater: the gold, or the
temple that makes the gold
sacred?
You also say, "If anyone swears
by the altar, it means nothing; but
if anyone swears by the gift on it,
he is bound by his oath."
You blind men! Which is greater:
the gift, or the altar that makes the
gift sacred?
Therefore, he who swears
by the altar swears by it and by
everything on it.
And he who swears
by the temple swears by it and by
the one who dwells in it.
And he who swears
by heaven swears by God's throne
and by the one who sits on it.

Woe to you,
teachers of the law
and Pharisees, you hypocrites!
You give a tenth of your
spices—mint, dill and cummin.
But you have neglected the
more important matters of the
law—justice, mercy and
faithfulness. You should have
practiced the latter, without
neglecting the former.

You blind guides!
You strain out a gnat
but swallow a camel.

Woe to you,
teachers of the law and
Pharisees, you hypocrites! You
clean the outside of the cup and
dish, but inside they are full of
greed and self-indulgence.
Blind Pharisee!
First clean the inside of the cup
and dish, and then the outside
also will be clean.

Woe to you,
teachers of the law and
Pharisees, you hypocrites! You
are like whitewashed tombs,
which look beautiful on the
outside but on the inside are full
of dead men's bones and
everything unclean.
In the same way, on the outside
you appear to people as
righteous but on the inside you
are full of hypocrisy and
wickedness.

Woe to you,
teachers of the law and
Pharisees, you hypocrites! You
build tombs for the prophets
and decorate the graves of the
righteous.
And you say, "If we had lived
in the days of our forefathers,
we would not have taken part
with them in shedding the
blood of the prophets."
So you testify against
yourselves that you are the
descendants of those who
murdered the prophets.
Fill up, then,
the measure of the sin
of your forefathers!

You snakes!
You brood of vipers!
How will you escape being
condemned to hell?
Therefore
I am sending you prophets and
wise men and teachers.
Some of them you will kill
and crucify;
others you will flog in your
synagogues and pursue from
town to town.
And so upon you will come all
the righteous blood that has
been shed on earth,
from the blood of righteous
Abel to the blood of Zechariah
son of Berekiah, whom you
murdered between the temple
and the altar.
I tell you the truth,
all this will come upon this
generation.

Jesus Laments over Jerusalem

Matthew 23:37-39

O Jerusalem,
Jerusalem,
you who kill the prophets
and stone those
sent to you,
how often I have longed
to gather your children
together,
as a hen
gathers her chicks
under her wings, but you
were not willing.
Look,
your house is left
to you desolate.

For I tell you,
you will not see me again
until you say,

"Blessed is he
who comes in the
name
of the Lord."

45

Signs of the End of the Age

Matthew 24:1-14

Jesus left the temple and was walking away
when his disciples came up to him
to call his attention to its buildings.
Do you see all these things?
he asked.
*I tell you the truth, not one stone here will be left on
another; every one will be thrown down.*

As Jesus was sitting on the Mount of Olives, the
disciples came to him privately. "Tell us," they said,
"when will this happen, and what will be the sign of
your coming and of the end of the age?"
Jesus answered:
*Watch out that no one deceives you.
For many will come in my name, claiming,
"I am the Christ," and will deceive many.*

*You will hear of wars and rumors of wars,
but see to it that you are not alarmed.
Such things must happen, but the end
is still to come.*

*Nation will rise against nation, and kingdom against
kingdom. There will be famines
and earthquakes in various places.
All these are the beginning of birth pains.*

*Then you will be handed over to be persecuted and
put to death, and you will be hated
by all nations because of me.*

*At that time many will turn away from the faith and
will betray and hate each other,
and many false prophets will appear
and deceive many people.
Because of the increase of wickedness, the love
of most will grow cold, but he who stands
firm to the end will be saved.*

**And this gospel of the kingdom will be preached
in the whole world as a testimony to all
nations, and then the end will come.**

The Great Tribulation

Matthew 24:15-28

So when you see standing in the holy place "the abomination that causes desolation," spoken of through the prophet Daniel—
let the reader understand—
then let those who are in Judea
flee to the mountains.
Let no one on the roof of his house
go down to take anything out of the house.
Let no one in the field go back to get his cloak.

How dreadful it will be in those days for pregnant women and nursing mothers!
Pray that your flight will not take place in winter or on the Sabbath.

For then there will be great distress, unequaled from the beginning of the world until now—and never to be equaled again.
If those days had not been cut short, no one would survive, but for the sake of the elect those days will be shortened.
At that time if anyone says to you,
"Look, here is the Christ!" or, "There he is!"
do not believe it.
For false Christs and false prophets will appear and perform great signs and miracles to deceive even the elect—if that were possible.

See, I have told you ahead of time.
So if anyone tells you, "There he is, out in the desert," do not go out; or, "Here he is, in the inner rooms," do not believe it.
For as the lightning comes from the east and flashes to the west, so will be the coming of the Son of Man.
Wherever there is a carcass, there the vultures will gather.

The Coming of the Son of Man

Matthew 24:29-31

Immediately after the distress of
those days
**"the sun will be darkened,
and the moon
will not give its light;
the stars will fall from the sky,
and the heavenly bodies
will be shaken."**
At that time the sign of the Son of
Man will appear in the sky,
and all the nations of the earth will
mourn. They will see the Son of Man
coming on the clouds of the sky, with
power and great glory.
And he will send his angels with a
loud trumpet call, and they will
gather his elect from the four winds,
from one end of the heavens to the
other.

The Parable of the Fig Tree

Matthew 24:32-35

Now learn this lesson from the fig
tree: As soon as its twigs get tender
and its leaves come out, you know
that summer is near.
Even so, when you see all these
things, you know that it is near, right
at the door.
I tell you the truth, this generation
will certainly not pass away until all
these things have happened.
Heaven and earth will pass away,
but my words will never
pass away.

51

The Faithful Servant and the Evil Servant

Matthew 24:45-51

*Who then is the faithful and wise servant,
whom the master has put in charge of the servants in his household to give them their food at the proper time?*

*It will be good for that servant whose master finds him doing so when he returns.
I tell you the truth,
he will put him in charge of all his possessions.
But suppose that servant is wicked and says to himself,
"My master is staying away a long time,"
and he then begins
to beat his fellow servants and to eat and drink with drunkards.
The master of that servant will come on a day
when he does not expect him and at an hour he is not aware of.*

**He will cut him
to pieces and assign him
a place with the
hypocrites,
where there will be
weeping and gnashing of
teeth.**

The Last Supper

Luke 22:7-22

Then came the day of Unleavened Bread
on which the Passover lamb had to be sacrificed.
Jesus sent Peter and John, saying,
*Go and make preparations for us to eat the
Passover.*
"Where do you want us to prepare for it?" they asked.
He replied,
*As you enter the city, a man carrying a jar of
water will meet you.
Follow him to the house that he enters,
and say to the owner of the house,
"The Teacher asks:
Where is the guest room, where I may eat the
Passover with my disciples?"
He will show you a large upper room, all
furnished. Make preparations there.*
They left and found things just as Jesus had told
them. So they prepared the Passover.
When the hour came, Jesus and his apostles reclined
at the table. And he said to them,
*I have eagerly desired to eat this Passover with
you before I suffer.
For I tell you, I will not eat it again until it finds
fulfillment in the kingdom of God.*
After taking the cup, he gave thanks and said,
*Take this and divide it among you.
For I tell you I will not drink again of the fruit of the
vine until the kingdom of God comes.*
And he took bread, gave thanks and broke it, and
gave it to them, saying,
**This is my body given for you; do this in
remembrance of me.**
In the same way, after the supper he took the cup,
saying,
**This cup is the new covenant in my blood,
which is poured out for you.**
*But the hand of him who is going to betray me is
with mine on the table.
The Son of Man will go as it has been decreed,
but woe to that man who betrays him.*

The Disciples Argue about Greatness

Luke 22:23-30

They began to question
among themselves which of
them it might be who would do
this. Also a dispute arose among
them as to which of them was
considered to be greatest.
Jesus said to them,
*The kings of the Gentiles
lord it over them; and those
who exercise authority over
them call themselves
Benefactors.
But you are not to be like that.
Instead, the greatest among
you should be like the
youngest, and the one who
rules like the one who serves.
For who is greater,
the one who is at the table or
the one who serves?
Is it not the one who is at the
table?*
**But I am among you as one
who serves.**
*You are those who have stood
by me in my trials.
And I confer on you a kingdom,
just as my Father conferred
one on me,
so that you may eat and drink
at my table in my kingdom and
sit on thrones,
judging the twelve tribes of
Israel.*

Jesus Predicts Peter's Denial

Luke 22:31-34

Simon, Simon,
Satan has asked
to sift you as
wheat.
But I have prayed
for you Simon,
that your faith
may not fail.
And when you
have turned back,
strengthen your
brothers.
But he replied,
"Lord, I am ready
to go with you to
prison and to
death."
Jesus answered,
I tell you,
Peter, before the
rooster crows
today,
you will deny
three times that
you know me.

Supplies for the Road

Luke 22:35-38

Then Jesus asked
them,
*When I sent you
without purse, bag
or sandals, did you
lack anything?*

"Nothing," they
answered.
He said to them,
*But now if you
have a purse,
take it,
and also a bag; and
if you don't have a
sword,
sell your cloak and
buy one.
It is written:*
**"And he was
numbered
with the
transgressors"** ;
*and I tell you that
this must be
fulfilled in me.
Yes, what is written
about me is
reaching its
fulfillment.*
The disciples said,
"See, Lord, here are
two swords."
*That is enough,
he replied.*

The King on a Cross

Luke 23:28-31

Jesus turned
and said to them,
*Daughters of Jerusalem,
do not weep for me;
weep for yourselves and for
your children.
For the time will come
when you will say,
"Blessed
are the barren women,
the wombs that never bore and
the breasts that never nursed!"
Then "they will say to the
mountains,
'Fall on us!' and to the hills,
'Cover us!' "
For if men do these things
when the tree is green, what
will happen when it is dry?*

Luke 23:34

Jesus said,
**Father, forgive them,
for they do not know what
they are doing.**
And they divided up his clothes
by casting lots.

Luke 23:43

Jesus answered him,
*I tell you the truth, today you
will be with me in paradise.*

Luke 23:46

Jesus called out with a loud
voice,
*Father, into your hands I
commit my spirit.*
When he had said this, he
breathed his last.

The Great Commission

Mark 16:15-18

He said to them,
**Go into all the world
and preach the good news
to all creation.**
Whoever believes and is baptized
will be saved, but whoever does not
believe will be condemned.
**And these signs
will accompany those
who believe:**
In my name
they will drive out demons;
they will speak in new tongues;
they will pick up snakes
with their hands;
and when they drink deadly poison,
it will not hurt them at all;
they will place their hands on sick
people, and they will get well.

Matthew 28:18-20

Then Jesus came to them and said,
**All authority
in heaven and on earth
has been given to me.
Therefore
go and make disciples
of all nations,
baptizing
them in the name
of the Father
and of the Son and of the
Holy Spirit,
and teaching them
to obey everything
I have commanded you.
And surely I will be with you
always, to the very end
of the age.**

The Scriptures Opened

Luke 24:44-49

He said to them,

*This is what I told you while
I was still with you:
Everything must be fulfilled
that is written about me in
the Law of Moses,
the Prophets, and the
Psalms.*
Then he opened their minds
so they could understand the
Scriptures.

He told them,
*This is what is written:
The Christ will suffer and
rise from the dead on the
third day,
and repentance and
forgiveness of sins will be
preached in his name to all
nations, beginning at
Jerusalem.
You are witnesses of these
things.*

**I am going to send you
what my Father has
promised;
but stay in the city until
you have been clothed
with power from on high.**

Photos by: Page:
     Pictor: 12–13, 22–23, 26–27, 30–31, 32–33, 36–37, 40–41, 42–43, 54–55, 56–57.
Tony Stone: Cover, 6–7, 10–11, 14–15, 16–17, 28–29, 34–35, 38–39, 46–47, 58–59,
             60–61, 62–63, back cover.
Image Bank: 8–9, 44–45, 48–49, 50–51.
      Huber: 4–5, 18–19, 20–21, 24–25, 52–53.